Thou
Musings of a
Nobody

Peter Davis

BookLeaf
Publishing

Thoughts and Musings of a Nobody © 2022
Peter Davis

All rights reserved.

Peter Davis asserts the moral right to be
identified as author of this work.

Presentation by *BookLeaf Publishing*

Web: www.bookleafpub.com

E-mail: info@bookleafpub.com

ISBN: 9789395621236

First edition 2022

DEDICATION

I dedicate this to the rock and foundation of everything good and positive in my life, my wife Rachel, without whom I would not have achieved half of what we have together, including our two wonderful children. I love you, Forever and Always. xx

PREFACE

I have written for as long as I can remember in a
range of fields - short plays, novels, sketches
and poems. To me, writing was always a step
away from reality, an escape into the other, a
place where I was free to express the thoughts
and feelings that otherwise would have been
quashed.

The poems in this book cover a long period
going back over 10 years, and were written
during a period of massive change in my life,
moving from one that was fraught, traumatic and
confrontational to one that is peaceful, happy
and loving. The poems in this collection reflects
the changes and transformations that occurred,
and as such, some poems may seem dark or
stressful. It is nice to read those and realise that
the dark time that is so evident in the writing has
now passed, and I hope the same for anyone
who cares to read them.

The empty theatre

I stand in the empty theatre

With it's ancient dusty smell,

The echo of the empty stage

Which dreams and wonders tell

The tinny sound of ivory keys

Sitting in the corner

The spacious house with history

Ten thousand past performers

A set goes up in one week's time

With actors tripping 'round

It goes back down in even less

Then starts another round

The empty dressing room is heavy

With a musty smell

Of make-up and of time gone by,

A thousand "weeks of hell"

The building echoes in it's mass

As a show begins

But then comes what will make it all worthwhile

In the very end

The empty chairs are filled within

An hour of unlocked doors

The talk is of the weather and

Of shows they'd seen before.

A silence falls across the house,

The actors' heartbeat skips

The curtain rises majestically

The tech crews grit their lips

The show goes on, with hitch or no

A separate yet collaborative work

The dance of sound and lights and crews

As sets change in the dark

The ever worried, coffee filled

Stage manager gives their cues

And when the curtain falls again

All listen for the news

A clap, a roar, a standing row,

A silence dead as night?

A shriek for "encore!", or applause

Will the show take flight?

Afterwards, while actors mingle

Among remaining crowds

And all the techs reset the cues

And directors unfurl their brows

The house then empties once again

With echoes, all that's left

Until another show begins

In the silenced deft

At this time, as before

In a voice too quiet to be heard

Says, "Thank you," to the empty stage

Then leaves without a word

It's impossible to explain

The pull of this, the theatre

But my soul is part of it's

Never-ending grandeur

It speaks to me, and calls my name

And this I will always know

That this is truly home for me

Forever, on with the show!

Love is

Real love is the look in someone's eyes
that is meant for you alone,
a gentle kiss that says everything will be okay,
a hand held in just the right way
at just the right time.

Real love is a secret told by one heart
and guarded by another,
a belief that someone knows you
as no one else can,
the little day-to-day acts of thoughtfulness
that go unmentioned but not unnoticed.

Rain

Softly falling down
each drop a symphony of sound
as it hits the tin roof
tap . . . tap . . . tap.

It can sound just like a sad song with a slow beat
the kind that makes you daydream
and feel sad and sigh
as you think of what might have been or could
be in your life.

Or maybe it is a happy song that brings back
sweet memories
tender thoughts and special smiles
thinking of someone who makes your heart beat
faster
and your laughter ring with happiness and joy.

Or maybe it is a love song
with sweet and soft lyrics
tender and romantic and sensual
that makes you think of dancing in the rain.

Only you can decide which song
is the one you are hearing

which music soothes your soul
and which song you want to sing along with.

Sometimes, you have to choose a song ...
and it isn't always easy.

Grateful

I write, its my light,
how i fight for my right,
to be me and not you
and its all i can do
to be fine and okay
and believe what i say
but i cant and i wont
its never do but just dont
and it hurts and i bleed
but all that i need
is that smile or that face
to put me back in my place
and back on my feet,
but all who i meet
wont look me in the eye
and i just want to die
but i wont give up yet
and ill never forget
those who struggled and tried
and sat with me when i just cried
who told me to get up and stand
and reached out their soft hand
to bring me back in the game
no matter how close i just came
to going out of the door

and walking over the floor
just going out on my own
with no cards and no phone
for day after day
just running away...

And I thank you for this,
Not with a hug or a kiss
But the way I know how:
So right here and right now,
This poor rhyme is for you,
And whatever we do,
I'll never forget
The way that we met,
Or the things that you do
That make you just you,
That help me be just me,
And i always will be

Grateful..

Live

Everyone know how varied life can be. Sometimes it's amazing and exciting, with surprises of noises and colour around every corner. When light never seems to fade and every new experience is something to treasure, to cling to.

And then there are times when the clouds never to seem to rise, when no matter how hard you try, you can never seem to keep a grasp of those things you cherish so much, and you feel as if life will never allow you to live.

But it does. And no matter how you try to keep them, the pictures and memories of all those wonderful, magical scenes slowly fade until they become simple pictures in an album. And the fear and the trials, they slowly go too, although you never imagined they could. What was once such a terrifying fear, becomes nothing but a shadow over time, dissipating in the breeze.

But occasionally, for the fortunate few, someone comes into your life and changes it immediately. You can talk without words, you can feel without touching. Their words sooth and revive you, and their touch electrifies you. They are able to trace the scars on your soul with their eyes, and your shame, your fears, and your mistakes, they do not disgust them or make them turn away.

And you know, that even if you never meet that person ever again, you will never, ever forget them. No matter how far you travel or how slowly you age, they will remain with you always. Not as a photo in an abandoned book, not some distant recollection that surfaces occasionally through the waters of your memory, but as part of you. As vital as the blood in your veins or the air in your lungs. You could no more forget them than you could forget yourself.

If you are fortunate enough to meet one of those people, hold on to them, trust them. Love them. As they love you. For too many people let this angel, this wonder, fall from their hands, and spend the rest of their lives searching for them again only to settle in disappointment and regret. Live.

Friend

I never realised what it meant to have a real
friend,
That true companion, the one who'll be there at
the end.
The one who always listens but doesn't always
agree,
Who will tell you the truth no matter how hard it
might be.
The one who just giggles and laughs at your
lines,
And who knows what goes on in the depths of
your mind.
Who knows when to give you a big push or a
cheer,
Or a hug or a kiss or a kick in the rear.
And the one you can trust like no other person
here on this earth,
Who at last is the one helping you remember
self-worth
Who knows how you feel just by one token
look,
And can read you as easily as opening a book.
To whom there is so much that does not need to
be said,

But is known with a movement, or a soft look
instead.
That person that you can tell absolutely anything
to,
I never knew what true friendship meant...

Till I met you...

The path to hope

Hurt is a strange word.
It implies there is a solution, that things will get better,
Whether through a bandage, a word or a gentle kiss.
But sometimes, just sometimes, when you find yourself
In a mist of sadness, bemused and bewildered,
It's hard to remember just where the path back lies.

And as you stumble and trip through the cold, empty numbness,
Old voices start whispering.
Whispering words you thought you had banished,
Words that you had vowed never to hear again.
Dangerous words with dangerous meanings.
You have worked hard to forget them, worked hard to reject them,
You can never go back there again.

And so, with staggering feet, you drag your wounded body

Back up the bank into reality, turning sadness into determination,
Fear into stubbornness, tears into a mask of smiles and sarcasm.
And you find that path, you use that path, you walk that path.
The path to hope.

Live II

Run.
Everywhere.
Aimlessly.
Without worrying.
Without looking back.
For the freedom.
Run.

Play.
Without thinking.
Without planning.
With imagination.
With love.
With life.
Play.

Laugh.
Loudly.
Endlessly.
Innocently.
At yourself.
For yourself.
Laugh.

Be.
Crazy.
Funny.
Courageous.
Loving.
Yourself.
Be.

Live.
For yourself.
Helping others.
The way you want.
The way you need.
Your life.
Live.

I resign

I am hereby officially tendering my resignation
as an adult.
I have decided I would like to accept the
responsibilities of an 8-year-old again.
I want to go to McDonald's and think that it's a
four star restaurant.
I want to sail sticks across a fresh mud puddle
and make ripples with rocks.
I want to think M&Ms are better than money
because you can eat them.
I want to lie under a big oak tree and drink
lemonade with my friends on a hot summer day.
I want to return to a time when life was simple.
When all you knew were colours, multiplication
tables, and nursery rhymes, but that didn't bother
you, because you didn't know what you didn't
know and you didn't care.
All you knew was to be happy because you were
blissfully unaware of all the things that should
make you worried or upset.
I want to think the world is fair.
That everyone is honest and good.
I want to believe that anything is possible.

I want to be oblivious to the complexities of life and be overly excited by the little things again.
I want to live simple again.
I don't want my day to consist of computer crashes, mountains of paperwork, depressing news, how to survive more days in the month than there is money in the bank, bills, gossip, illness, and loss of loved ones.
I want to believe in the power of smiles, hugs, a kind word, truth, justice, peace, dreams, the imagination, mankind, and making angels in the snow.
So... here's my chequebook and my car keys, my credit cards and all my responsibility.
I am officially resigning from adulthood.
And if you want to discuss this further, you'll have to catch me first, 'cause,
"Tag! You're it."

Today

I told today.
I told of dark twisted secrets, of fears,
Of long hidden failures and of a little girl's tears.
I told something that I swore was never going to
be said,
A secret best buried till after I'm dead.

I told today.
Yet the person I told just listened and sighed,
And held me and kissed my cheeks while I
cried,
And said 'I told you before, no matter what, I am
here'
And picked me right up and cuddled me near.

And the fear, and the panic, the stress and alarm,
Faded fast right away and I suddenly felt calm.
And the years of self-hate and sadness and guilt,
While still there deep inside, subsided, if just for
a bit.

For I should have known, for me, she would still
be right there,
With that twinkle for me to show that she does
care.

I can't thank her enough for making me feel how
I do,
But I hope over time, I can help her feel this way
too.

Sit by the fire

Come sit by the fire,
And talk awhile,
And I'll tell you what I miss.
Your loving eyes,
Your tender smile,
The passion in your kiss.

Come sit by the fire,
And stay awhile.
Our story must be told -
The magic of
Your tenderness,
Strikes my very soul.

Come walk with me,
And take my hand,
Together we will be,
As we go walking
On the sand,
Serenaded by the sea.

Come stay with me,
And be my love,
And together we will see
That happiness and peacefulness
Are meant for you and me

I'm known for the words

I'm known for the words
That I put on the page,
And I'm famous for never
Quite acting my age,
And if it's a laugh that you want,
Or advice from the soul,
You know where to come,
Whatever your goal.
For I am here for you all,
And always will be,
To help you smile or relax,
But who is there for me?
When at night when I feel,
That I'm seven again,
When I shiver and shake,
And can't move where I'm lain,
When I shout out at night,
And roll around in my bed.
When it all gets too much,
And I wish I was dead,
When I cant sleep for months,
Or even just rest,
When my brain turns to mush
And I don't know what's best,
To do for myself,

To stay here or run,
And I think things are over
Before they've begun.
When I can't trust or believe,
The words that they say,
And think it's only a joke,
That they will leave me today.
But it's me, and I can't
Let everyone down,
I have to been seen to stand up,
And cover my frown.
So I'll be the guy that you need,
I'll hide the scars and the fears,
I'll always be here,
To mop up your tears.
I'll be your teacher,
Your boyfriend, your family or friend,
But answer this question,
Please, when does it end?

On the swings

Forward....back
Forward....back
I watch as your spirits rise,
The light return to your eyes.
A smile creeps back on your face,
Your mind away from the scary place.
You turn to me and I understand,
All I want to do is hold your hand,
And let you know you are safe with me
For now and always will be.
But for now, you lean back and go even higher,
A smile on your lips and your soul on fire,
Released, free, as one with the air,
And I hope you know how much I do care...

Fear

I used to stand upon tall ladders
And look down to the depths below
Wondering what all the fuss was
If I should fall.

My mother said "Get down!"
My brother just cried,
While I stood on the very highest step
Where the words "No Step" reside.

I didn't conceive what was at risk,
I thought it was just life
And life wasn't that big of a deal
At least not to me.

I used to walk across high bridges
And ponder what it would be to fly
To soar for a moment or two.
If I should stumble.

My eyes must have deceived me as
Many a stranger paused
To watch,
Me. Watch the water.
The swirls which mesmerized my mind.

I didn't give it much a thought,
The fall that is
As it would end in darkness
A lack of light
And I would know nothing. Anymore.

I used to drive my car
At night
And wonder what it would be like to cross that
line.
The white one.
On the side.

What it would be like to fall asleep and sail,
For a second or two,
To never know what happened.
To never awake.

It really didn't worry me that much
It only meant no more thoughts,
No more strain
Of life.
Only rest.

But now I stand upon the lowest rung,
I walk along the shortest bridge,
And drive the most deserted roads
In fear.

For now I find myself afraid to die.
Terrified of no thought.
Fearful of no consciousness.
Scared of the most timid danger.

For now I finally know what it means to live.

The day before my birthday

When you are a kid, you can't wait for your
birthday,
And all the fun stuff that it brings,
Like the cake, the parties and presents,
And the other cool things.

But when you are older, the day ain't so special,
In fact it's a day that is just like the rest.
But I don't care because I have a new secret,
And I don't need to be down or depressed.

Cos I don't really care about birthdays,
They come around every year,
But the day that's the day before my birthday,
Now that's the one that will I hold dear.

Just to spend the day not pretending,
To be myself and have a smile on my face.
To share it with the person that matters,
And to be in a happier place.

To just wander around without direction,
And to enjoy all the things that we see,
Just laughing, and loving and joking,
And being able to show the real me.

Cos I don't really care about birthdays,
They come around every year,
But the day that's the day before my birthday,
That's the one that I will hold dear

So cakes with lit candles, you can keep 'em
And I really don't need a surprise.
All I want is what I had yesterday,
The look that I saw in her eyes.

So next year, you can save your good wishes,
The ninth will be the same as the rest.
So thank you all, but I really don't need them,
For it is the eigth that is always the best.

Cos I don't really care about birthdays,
They come around every year,
But the day that's the day before my birthday,
That's the one that I will hold dear.

Being a Dad

All Dads are great at building. Fixing any household issue with nothing more than skill and duct tape.

Except I can't.

And all Dads are excellent drivers and have an encyclopedic knowledge of cars, engines and all things motoring.

Except I don't.

And all Dads know everything about sports - the teams, the players, the stats, and can quote seminal matches play by play.

Except I can't.

What I can do is give you a world of magic, of imagination and wonder.

i can create stories with you in the title role, and lead you on countless adventures.

I can show you the magic of theatre, the wonder that audiences feel and the skills needed to make it happen.

But most of all, I will love you. I will be here to guard you and protect you for the rest of my days.

Because it is not the skills or knowledge that make a father. It's the journey of learning together and that makes me the father I am and the father I want to be.

Getting Old

When i get old...

I will have to stop drinking at lunchtime, else
sleep all afternoon.
I will find excuses not to go to parties and
instead sit at home with a movie and my wife.
I will make funny noises every time i stand up or
sit down, as if they help the physical process.
I will patiently watch Youtube videos with my
son and realise that my knowledge of pop
culture is now on a par with when I tried to
explain to my parents what a Pet Shop Boy was.
I will shudder at the thought of drinking all night
and going to a hot, sweaty club where there are
no seats and you can't hear anyone speak.
I will gladly swop spending vast amounts of
money on dubious nights out and will instead
spend vast amounts of money in deli's and
grocery stores.
I... got old

Read

I once got asked, 'What are you reading for?'
Not 'what are you reading?' but 'why?'

Not reading is like not breathing. Everyone
should, no must read. Read anything.
Everything.
Read good books, trashy books, factual books,
fantasy books. Read books about people, about
lives, about journeys, about things that happened
and things that didn't. About things that matter
and things that don't. Read comic books, art
books, classic books, 'good' books and 'bad'
books.
Books that make you smile, that make you cry,
that make you angry. Books that stir your
imagination, your fascination and your hunger
for the unknown.
Without books, we have no knowledge or
imagination. With no knowledge or imagination,
we are nothing.
Read